THE SAGA
Ancient and Ours

The Story of Adam, Eve, and the Serpent—
Then and Now

Timothy Vagus

Published by Oxbow Lake

P.O. Box 175, Englewood, CO 80151

The Saga: Ancient and Ours

Copyright © 2018, By Timothy Vagus

www.timothyvagus.com

ISBN-978-1-945413-05-6

10 9 8 7 6 5 4 3 2 1

Any faults in this book belong to the author.

Credit for whatever is true and helpful belongs elsewhere.

Wisdom cries out in the streets;
She shouts in public places. ...
Never let go of kindness and truth.
Tie them around your neck;
Engrave them on your heart!

Translated by the author from the ancient Hebrew book
Mishlei, "Proverbs" 1:20 and 3:3

Contents

A Word from the Author

This book was born in jail, the result of my chaplain service to incarcerated men. Their experiences were entirely foreign to me. Though I'd lived in numerous countries and learned several languages, I struggled to connect with Americans in jail. Temporarily locked up with them, I was more locked up within. What do we have in common? What should I say or not say? What will make sense of their lives and offer them hope?

Genesis chapter 3, understood as a metaphor, not only bridged the gap between us, it changed our lives together. We found ourselves in a mysterious but strangely familiar world. I'd known the story for decades but hadn't grasped its deeper meanings. Looking at them together, we've cried, laughed, considered our past, and renewed our hope for the future.

I've discussed the story with small groups of inmates, some two thousand men, over the last six years. You, too, are welcome to "The Saga."

Timothy Vagus, former atheist and lifelong wanderer

Preface

Yes, this book was born in jail. Though most people have never been there, don't we all at times sense a kind of imprisonment, the bars of fear, regret, confusion, unmet longing, or even impending death? Aren't we all locked up? When we feel that way and look for something better, we become like brave inmates seeking a new start.

Everyone loves a good story. A saga is even better—vast, ageless, and unbounded by its own history. Looming before us, front door ajar and inviting, it welcomes whoever steps within.

Children have hungry imaginations. When told a story, they enter it naturally. We more mature and stable types tend to focus on the material, the useful, and the here and now. In practice that often means we just scurry about in a micro-orbit we call our life. In that small, familiar place we can protect what's at hand, but we may lose something larger.

The Saga beckons us elsewhere, inviting us to walk the paths of a profound and ancient account.

To venture in, we needn't settle debates about its historicity. A metaphorical approach neither precludes nor requires a position about the primeval facts. The story's messages and mysteries stand as the foundation of Judaism, Christianity, and Islam, as a centerpiece in the world's cultural treasury, and as the muse of great philosophers, scientists, politicians, and artists.

Wisdom tells us all, whether we are skeptics, seekers, or religious, to enter, linger, and gaze. When we do, we find ourselves surrounded by compelling vistas, thrilling and disturbing, unsettled and still, frightful yet offering hope. Life's most pressing questions encircle us in the story's few short events.

Some of you may respond that this little book reads in too much. In places it probably does. But sagas beg to be explored. They are purposely rich, deep, and metaphorical, prodding us toward reflection and application. In this way the Bible's drama has spoken not only through the millennia, it appeals to us today. For here we find the substance of faith, not like some clouds shielding weak eyes from a bright sun, but the archeological remains of our human psyche and experience.

The Biblical selection used as the backbone was translated afresh by the author from the ancient Hebrew text. More about this can be found in the appendix. Readers may prefer a different translation, and are welcome to base their reading upon it.

Finally, what follows is certainly not the last word. Before us emerges something grander than any one person can perceive or describe. Add your own insights to the treasures. And may my fellow travelers be challenged and encouraged, whether we stumble through life or imagine ourselves stout and brave.

Chapter 1: Problems in Paradise

Of all the animals the Eternal God made, the serpent was the most cunning. And he asked the woman, "Can it be? Did God actually say, 'You two must not eat from any of the garden trees'?"[1]

This outlandish little book invites you to imagine. We all let ourselves be lured into the world of a movie or novel. Opinions about its history aside, this story's scenes will expand your experience. Once inside, you may even reconsider your own life's drama.

Imagine a heavy shipping crate jammed full of compressed rubber balls. To save most of the contents, you can't just pop the top. We'll bore into this story slowly, sentence by sentence and phrase by phrase. Sometimes, even a word will unfold before us into a landscape of ideas.

We begin with Adam and Eve. They live in what we call "paradise," a place not unlike our dreams

---

1 Notes about this translation are found in the Appendix.

today, whether a tropical island, a chateau in the Alps, or a cottage in the woods. When we observe animals, they often seem content. But we humans seek perfection. Happy children's fairy tales may lie behind us, but their aura remains visible in our quest for the finest. We want the best possible everything, and our list is long: health, finances, family, friends, society, education, home, car, food and drink, vacations, technology, entertainment, sports, clothing, government, ecology, or whatever. We still yearn, wistfully, to live "happily ever after." Sadly, reality seems so brutal. The past mocks us and the present constantly menaces, so why can't we simply banish longings for a perfect life? Our saga implies we were made for it.

Of all the animals the Eternal God made ...

Made?! We'll soon see how the first humans face problems even in paradise. But with that four-letter word "made" it is we who confront a problem they could never imagine. The unassuming phrase "the Eternal God made" raises a dust storm of debate about our origins, and it echoes our story's famous first words: "In the beginning ..." (Genesis 1:1).

Whatever our position about origins, most of us agree that long ago something started, something now exists, and we're somehow part of it.

Smart people have unveiled new worlds, from the stunning expanse of space to unimaginably tiny subatomic stuff. Large or small, it's all manipulated by the unseen powers that be. We hear of mass and gravity, electromagnetic radiation, particles and waves, forces enthroned like the ancient gods of Greece and Rome. We find ourselves in a deeply mysterious realm. Everything constantly whirls about, whether way out in space, on the winds and tides of our planet, in atomic orbits, and bogglingly complex, life beneath the dry, outermost layer of our skin. Our heart pumps relentlessly, our muscles tense and contract, our internal organs continually process food, water, air, and waste, our sense organs constantly monitor external stimuli, our hormones pass on basic directions, our nerves shoot out detailed instructions, and our brain buzzes like an electric beehive.

Buried in all that, making up our organs and tissues, is the prime unit of life. We call it a cell, as if it's a small, locked room. But it's far more than a little bag of protoplasmic jelly surrounding a nucleus, as scientists not long ago believed. Today they tell us that within every cell lives a self-replicating, interactive community of microscopic, biological machines. If we could shrink ourselves and walk through a door in a cell wall, we'd be engulfed by a domain so complex it makes our communication satellites seem like a stack of children's blocks.

Opposing the saga is our modern creation story. It teaches us to believe we arose not from intent or plan, but as if from an unmanned laboratory. During long lost millennia, the laboratory filled up with test tubes, Bunsen burners, and chemicals. Unplanned experiments went on continually. Most ended with broken glass and poisonous spills. But some must have been fruitful, for after all, life exists. Our modern story still has a beginning, but it leaves many of us uneasy. It makes us mere accidents, and we feel worse off for knowing it. If we were simply sea slugs, at least we wouldn't be troubled by such thoughts.

Many people prize their ancestry. Some go to great lengths researching it, seeking a link with the past and a place in the present. We want to know who we are. By our modern myth, if we really trace our parentage, we go back to those brainless beasts on the ocean floor. From there our ancient forebears by struggle and luck crawled out of their deep-sea test tubes. They survived new challenges on land and supplanted their peers. Gradually, and finally, voilà, here we are. But beyond all the chemicals and mindless experiments, are we really mere children of chance, orphans of the universe, biological blips destined to sink in the borderless sea of time?

To help me sort this out, I imagine a huge junkyard. Though obviously a big mess, all the necessary stuff is right there. But the situation calls for energy. So I pretend to bomb it now and then, here and there. Can I believe that given enough time and luck, even vast eons of time and stupendous luck, some obvious order will result, if only in a corner? That's hard. Not even the relatively simple mess of a teenager's room can ever bring itself to order. Parents have to challenge their kids, however grudgingly, to thoughtfully apply to the task their eyes, legs, arms, and hands.

But maybe my junkyard just needs more time. I add sun, wind, rain, and temperature changes to stir things up. And then still more time. And more. And even more still. Beyond mess and decay, will anything come of it? I'm having deep trouble believing. Opening the teenager's windows to a storm only makes things worse.

Noting the complexity of life and all that surrounds us, believing in chance and time requires an awful lot of faith. But even if I could somehow be persuaded by the modern creation story, I refuse to give it a hug. For I find myself longing for something else, something beyond just energy and particles and time. I want to be more than accidentally arranged junk.

However depressing or chilling, the soulish emptiness of the modern story doesn't make it wrong. But it bequeaths us nothing for the heart, leaving our prized humanity gutted like a fish for roasting. Some people imagine we can create meaning. We may be clever enough to discover new worlds, but we can't make something, meaning included, out of nothing. But doesn't the ancient view bring its own problems? If a greater being created us, we can't claim first place in the universe. We might even be watched and evaluated. That prospect may be frightening, but it offers dignity and hope, making us more than self-reflective sea slugs singing the blues.

Whatever the creative mechanism, many of us feel very uneasy with the ancient swamp and its haphazard experiments, with its unending death, temporary survivors, and eternal losers. We want purpose and significance. We want our lives and loves and striving and children to count for something. We want to be, somehow, more than molecular motion.

And so we face a fork in the road. Either direction involves faith. None of us witnessed the beginning. We must adopt a creed, whether it be mind-centered or mindless, whether a cosmos (ancient Greek for "order") generated by intelligence or a product of pure chance. Some of us may invent a third way, claiming it doesn't matter. But that, too, is a faith. There's no escaping from reason by entrusting ourselves to indifference.

Enough about origins. Our saga moves on in its first phrase. The adjective "Eternal," used to describe the term "God," implies the existence of yet another realm. Material objects are defined by movement (think ever-whizzing electrons) and thus by time. If something non-material existed first, by definition it would be outside of time. Science investigates the physical, but it doesn't do well with the metaphysical, with thought, meaning, purpose, spirit, or soul. Every material item has a beginning, but what about the immaterial? What about an immense, contemplative, eternal Soul?

Life isn't easy. Hard questions like these can make it worse. And just ahead the story may give us reason to reject any idea of an eternal being, especially a good one. For into paradise enters the serpent, and with it our lifelong outrage against evil.

... the serpent was the most cunning. And he asked the woman ...

The Hebrew word translated "cunning" is very similar to the Hebrew word meaning "naked," Adam and Eve's condition before the serpent shows up.[2] The selection of terms is clearly intentional. The couple has nothing to hide, so they feel no shame. To secure his purpose, the serpent has much to hide.

Prior to this, God called his creation "very good." We see the light, land and sea, vegetation, sun, moon and stars, animals in water and on land, and human beings. Though beautiful and without mistake, from its inception paradise is not unassailable. The creator had warned Adam about the possibility of death.[3] Only later does the serpent incite harm. The story claims he harms us still. But the potential for death was present from the start, with or without the beast.

That terrible possibility of death can be assessed from opposite directions. It was either intentional and by design, or it was a flaw in the product, an oversight, a deficiency in the creator's work. The

---

2 See Genesis 2:25.
3 See Genesis 2:17.

saga clearly claims the former. Death would result only by a deliberate decision. When the creator made Adam and Eve "in his own image,"[4] we're to understand that a measure of self-determination was a central component of their nature. We might label it the freedom to choose, moral responsibility, or the personal and even God-given right to stand with or against their maker. But for that divine right to become real and actually mean anything, they had to use it. They must face some significant alternatives and choose between them. But what? The creator had established eating as an enjoyable necessity. It became the perfect arena for the couple to sooner or later face their high calling. Will they eat or reject the fateful fruit?

We may ask why, if the creator is so great, he didn't make us both great-souled and unable to fail. Theoretically, as far as we can tell from here, he could have. On the other hand, that might be like expecting him to make a round square. Choice is either real and therefore dangerous, or it is nothing at all. And let's be honest. Having experienced freedom, how many of us would return it to the manufacturer? Even then, we would be choosing to reject choice, arguably an absurdity. We are stuck, or blessed, or whatever with the freedom we so often prize. Now we must deal with it.

Before we watch our forebears actuate their own freedom, let's note some important deductions,

---

4 See Genesis 1:26, 27.

implications, and speculations based upon what we've seen thus far.

First, the saga claims that our world intersects with another type of higher being. The serpent is clearly no mere animal. It talks. It knows about important things. It interacts with the woman like no other creature does. And as we'll see later, it makes assertions, encourages thought, calls for action, and incites rebellion. Beyond this part of Genesis, the Hebrew Scriptures point directly and indirectly to another realm of beings, the angelic-demonic.[5] If real, that realm could be responsible for at least some of what we describe as paranormal, alien, spiritual, supernatural, and the like. The saga takes place in a profound world, and far from diminishing our own, the story expands it and confounds us.

Second, the creator is ultimately responsible for the serpent's existence, but not necessarily for the state we first encounter him. We note that God had made a good world which later changed for the worse. Adam and Eve, though initially vibrant beings, were told they could die. A fair deduction, even if only based upon their limited understanding at that time, might be that the serpent had been created good but subsequently changed. After all, God had warned it could happen to them.

---

5 See, for instance, Genesis chapter 16, Deuteronomy 32:17, Isaiah 14:1-23, Ezekiel 28:1-19, Psalm 106:36-38, Job chapters one and two, and Daniel chapter 10.

Third, the creator presumably allows the serpent to enter the garden. Persuasive as he might be, at this point the beast can only talk. The possibility of horror in paradise existed beforehand. The serpent has no power to bring it about directly. The ultimate choice is up to the man and the woman, sovereigns of their domain. They could pose serpent-like questions without the aid of an insidious third party. Either way, our first people have to weigh their options. The serpent merely brings those options to the fore.

Finally, even if we class our story as divine revelation, truth we couldn't otherwise know, it didn't and still doesn't explain everything, whether for Adam and Eve, early readers of Genesis, or us today. It provides what we need to know but not always what we want to know. That, it seems, is meant for later.[6]

---

6 This section concludes with what may be a pesky footnote to some people but a major concern to others. The language used here follows the original Hebrew by speaking of God, the creator, in masculine terms, words like "he," "him," "his," and "himself." But the creator is not a man or a male. He made both Adam and Eve, male and female, in his "image" (Genesis 1:27). So the creator must be seen as somehow neuter, asexual, hermaphroditic, or something of that order. Readers are free to change the terminology. You can substitute all the male terms about God with equally inaccurate female terms. You can expand them by reading "s/he" and "him/her." You can join the surprisingly long list of people who've actually invented words like *hesh*, *shim*, *hirs*, and *hermself*. Or you can simplify things with "it," etc. I won't be offended, and hope my use of traditional forms likewise does not mislead or offend. Consider it an old convention, useful but distorted. Human language, whether Hebrew, English, or Esperanto, often fails when talking about a being beyond our experience.

"Can it be? Did God actually say, 'You two must not eat from any of the garden trees'?"

Questions can open doors to learning and truth, but they can also lead us off a cliff. Sadly, the world's first recorded question cloaks feigned surprise, baseless indignation, and a distortion of key facts. As we watch Eve consider all this, we owe her some sympathy. Though animals don't talk every day, and didn't even then, everything was still new. What she was challenged to consider, even as we are now, is the serpent's verbiage. Not a passing "Hello, ma'am" or "Have a nice day in paradise!" the serpent's inquiry introduces significant issues that require dissection.

Surprise. If we take the most innocent, Evian, approach, the serpent is either wrongly informed or forgetful. But his obvious surprise implies that he has an opinion. So we're to understand that he's hiding something, not merely parroting what he may have heard.

Indignation. Creators have the right to limit their creation, and the freedom God gives is very broad. He imposes only a single restraint. What if he had, in fact, forbidden eating from all trees? That would be his prerogative. The serpent, however, is a master marketer and a grasping politician. Though no problem exists, he manipulates his audience with a few soft words. He hopes that by breeding discontent, disillusionment, and indignation, he might bring the existing ruler to trial, damage his reputation, and destroy his work.

Distortion. The serpent focuses upon the world's single negative command.[7] He might have inquired about the nature of various animals and Adam's names for them,[8] the chronology of what God had created, the classification of plants and trees, or any number of topics. But it's a very dangerous game to misstate, intentionally or not, the lone edict in all creation which, if broken, unleashes disaster.

Though the serpent is cunning, his words betray him. Following all this from Eve's barefoot perspective, it's entirely fair to conclude that he is either foolish or malignant. This trespasser insinuates problems with Eve's benefactor and lures her into a dangerous position. If she lived in our messy, cynical world, experience might have better prepared her. She does, however, possess some divinely provided assets which we'll watch her use.

---

7 See Genesis 2:15, 16.
8 See Genesis 2:19-20.

Chapter 2: Choices

The woman responded, "We may eat fruit from the garden trees. But God did say, 'You two must not eat fruit from the tree in the middle, or even touch it. If you do, you will die.'"

We like choices. Our thoughts dreamily wander to restaurants serving great foods, on-line shopping options galore, or shoreline excursions on a Mediterranean cruise. Choosing between chest pain and heart surgery is not nearly so pleasant. Uncertainty follows us in our education, professions, jobs, health, finances, relationships, family, lifestyles, and politics. Life assails us, and our responses define us.

The woman responded ...

Eve's dream, like many of ours, might simply be to enjoy a charmed and relaxed life. If she had only plugged her ears to the serpent's questions! Now it is too late.

In fact, it was too late from the start. The tree itself is an intrusion. Placed by the creator in the middle of her world, it points to a realm beyond the physical. It calls for reflection and a response of the soul.

Big issues now confront Eve. She can trust the creator or she can trust the serpent. She might look to her instincts, but she doesn't know very much. Reality far exceeds her experience. A barrage of ideas disturbs her peace, mocking any glib or enchanted approach to an idyllic future. She faces questions and doubts about truth, personalities who vie for attention, and life and death staring back from eyeless masks. Yet Eve's options at this point are aggravatingly few. Though she didn't will herself into existence, it appears she can choose to end it. Neither did she write the rules, but she must either conform or oppose. Faith in something, whether this or that, is required even in paradise. She starts out on the path she knows.

"We may eat fruit from the garden trees."

Everyone likes fine food and good conversation. Together, they are near to bliss. A bit of reflection on this point is worth our time. Eve is talking about eating. The organs for each activity are nearly identical. An odd muscle in the middle is central to both. We eat first of all to live. (Though we sometimes live to eat.) To live well, we communicate. It's no coincidence that our saga opens with these essentials of life and society. Vast parts of our own world today cater to what enters and exits our mouths. We support massive industries of food production and preservation, commerce, communication, education, and government. In many ways, life revolves around our tongue. Divinely provided for survival, pleasure, community, and advancement, it can also deceive and kill. Such a strange and powerful little thing!

The first people may eat from the trees, which Eve and Adam no doubt do. But fruit is not merely a happy accident. It was designed for food and fun. Trees, which produce it, were designed for beauty, shade, and their part in an intricate biological system. As trees are central to maintaining life, one becomes central to understanding it. Though the first people don't possess choice over everything, they can order their affairs in myriad ways. This one tree allows them to decide the biggest issue of all— whether or not to continue with life as they know it.

"But God did say,"

Adam, Eve, and the serpent can all communicate. Eve asserts that God can too, and has. That's a massive claim, provocative both then and today. But if a great mind created, can it not also communicate? We may love the idea, doubt it, dismiss it, mock it, or hate it, but we cannot entirely avoid it. We stand, as it were, at an alpine crossing marked by a large, hewn pole. A sign on the top reads *Divine Truth?* Nailed underneath, jabbing out to mark diverse paths, are a half dozen pointers that read: *Impossible, Maybe, Irrelevant, Wonderful, Illusion, Evil.* Our lives venture out from there, intentionally or not, one way or another.

Listening to Eve quote the divine authority, we may judge her as naïve. In fact, although we imagine ourselves independent thinkers, we can't produce a meaningful sentence if we've never lived in society, the place where language is now acquired. We all depend upon our predecessors.

A modern Mowgli-like girl, surviving basically with dogs, was documented to have a vocabulary of only two words, "yes" and "no." That was all she had learned from her alcoholic mother, who had essentially abandoned her. Take the story as you wish, but the point remains: directly and indirectly we learn from people. They, in turn, reflect a long history of human experience. Our lives, thoughts, and very nature are bound up with our ancestors. We are all, as the poet Donne wrote, "a piece of the continent, a part of the main."

Neither can we imagine a meaningful life without truth and hope. We make observations and defend our convictions. We cherish self-worth and believe life has purpose. Absent that, we move toward depression, escapism, and death. But how can real significance simply crawl, along with our purported ancestors, out of evolution's ancient seas and swamps? Our hearts require more than biology provides.

We may feel that the only voice from afar is that of our own echo. If so, our final conclusion about truth will be, "There is no truth." But that claim is no mere whimper. Like its opposite, it stands equally massive and with profound implications. If we face it squarely, doesn't the lack of truth melt our hopes into watery self-confidence? Don't we just devolve into rats running through a maze without exit or prize? If, however, a great being has somehow created, might we not trust that, like a great painter, sculptor, or musician, he also communicates, at least through his art? Might he also speak in history or to our own inner being? If so, the rat-like maze of our existence might have a portal and our lives acquire meaning. Our tongue would then be capable of something truly significant. With that hope in view, Eve recalls and cites her maker.

"'You two must not eat fruit from the tree in the middle, or even touch it. If you do, you will die.'"

Some will cry foul. "There he goes again! Right from the start, God telling people what not to do, and so on ad nauseam throughout history!" But is such a caricature fair? Along with the gift of many happy choices, a restriction of one kind or another may be as necessary to freedom as hate is to love. Without something to reject, we have no real freedom to accept. Further along in our saga the world will change. New orders will become necessary. But at this point, the lone command to the first people should be viewed as an opportunity, both wonderful and dangerous.

We expect our own laws to be carefully worded. Slight alterations can change our lives. Eve cites her trusted authority, but does so inaccurately. According to the earlier record, God never said anything about touching the fruit.[9] There's only one law in paradise.

---

9 See Genesis 2:17.

It shouldn't be hard to get it right, especially when neglecting it can be deadly. The consequences of that neglect will surface later.

Even our own secular political leaders talk of an "arc" of the "moral universe" that "bends toward justice." But if the universe arose by chance, don't morality and justice belong to fairy tales? Stalin and Mao, history's most voracious murderers, were atheists. From their point of view, they were apparently the wisest, strongest, and fittest members of the species who rightly eliminated wrong-headed opposition. But talk like that embarrasses even most atheists. So it seems quite clear that somehow, morality is stamped upon our psyche and marches forth with our genes. In the communist creed, Stalin and Mao actually relied upon a moral dictum of Karl Marx: "From each according to his ability, to each according to his needs." We cannot manage without do's and don'ts. Our saga and our hearts point to a justice greater than expedience, preference, self, or even society. Putting all this succinctly in somewhat dated English, "Whence the moral voice if not a great, good Soul?"

Finally, Eve might do better than simply answer the serpent's questions. Complying with his expectations makes her vulnerable. Questioning the serpent in response would level the field. "Who are you?" "Why do you mention my provider?" "What have you ever done for me?" "What's in this for you?" But because Eve plays the serpent's game, he can raise the stakes. And he does.

Chapter 3: Revolution

"You absolutely will not die!" the serpent replied. "For God himself knows that the moment you two eat from it your eyes will be opened. You will be like God, enlightened about good and bad, right and wrong!"[10]

The Serpent's History

The serpent begins by asking Eve seemingly innocuous questions. He ends by publishing scandalous, earth-shattering headlines: *God's a liar! Stays on top by depriving you!* Since that time, for one reason or another, not a few people have believed the bad press.

The serpent's words imply events which occurred elsewhere, whether before our saga or concurrent but outside. Though the details are not available here, the outcome is plain. God made all things "good." At a minimum, that means "functioning according to plan." The serpent works against those plans, and

---

10 Notes about this translation are found in the Appendix.

therefore must have changed. Though now at odds with one another, each of those two great beings agree on one thing: if Adam and Eve eat the fruit, they will undergo enormous change. That prospect has stood front and center from the start. Creation is wonderful, but it is vulnerable.

So we see that the serpent (more accurately, the being which appears as a serpent) steps on earth's stage with a history, one which culminated in opposition to his creator. The first revolutionary now calls Eve to join him. Clearly not a mere animal, he infiltrates the human realm in the form of a subservient creature. He's armed with experience, and may have already begun elsewhere what he suggests to Eve on earth. Meanwhile, the creator stands off to the side, allowing everyone to express the freedom he grants. But he does limit the serpent's weaponry. Though permitted to descend upon the planet, at this point he is only allowed to talk. Because the man and the woman are earth's masters,[11] they alone can choose to alter its fate. The tree is the focal point.

Frankly, this story reflects typical sci-fi plots. But it's more accurate to say that sci-fi plots reflect the story. Our saga far surpasses its popular, dream-world descendants. Not only was it written long before, its content does more than simply rattle our seats. It shakes and unsettles our deepest selves. For what follows depicts not just events in another place, but those in our world today. Deeper and more

11 See Genesis 1:26-31.

unsettling still will be its description of our own hearts.

We move on to ask if the serpent's proposed revolution is justified. It begins, like all revolutions do, with expressions of discontent. As noted, the serpent is permitted only to talk, but he does so with great care and power. The little muscle in his mouth wields his sword, and the devil is in the details.

The Serpent's Words

Given the high stakes, the serpent's shocking assertions, and the fact that his ideas are entirely new to Eve, she would do well to scrutinize what he says. And so would we, reminding ourselves that even falsehood contains a measure of truth.

... not die ...

Eve may well have little experience with death. She might or might not have seen animals pass away. But based on the confines of the story, all we can be sure of is that she and Adam had ended the life of certain plants, or at least the parts which they had eaten.

We may believe our experience is superior to hers, but death is strange to us even today. At the lowest level, many things "die." We use the word to describe what happens to computers, cars, superstitions, and ambitions. Though we still end plant life, only some is for food. Large amounts go toward fuel, clothing, medicine, and industrial applications.

But what does it mean for a person to die? Though we understand the basic physical manifestations, even they retain some ambiguity. Beyond the physical, people throughout history have believed that something spiritual lives on. That may be impossible to prove, but post-mortem nothingness is also impossible to prove. We can only believe, or believe not, that spiritual life survives. It's frightening to think that death endures forever. Most people hope, or at least want, for something good to follow. Such a desire might imply we are weak, unable to face reality. But it might also imply we were made for eternity. Skeptics who try to beat that idea out of human heads work in a field with long-term job security.

What if the order is reversed? Can a spiritual part of us die before our body? Again, we don't have direct proof, but note, for example, how we describe a debilitating loss: "When her child passed away, something in her died." Still closer to spiritual death is a mind which stops working normally. Physical trauma, oxygen deprivation, or age-related diseases of the brain can seemingly kill the vibrant person who once was. The body becomes a breathing shell. For surviving loved ones, that can be worse than physical death.

In summary, when the creator and the serpent speak of death, they might well be referring to different things, and purposely so.

... God himself knows ... You will be like God ...

Consistent with the headlines in the serpent's newspaper, it's very possible that God wants to stay on top. Would that be right, wrong, or a necessity? The answer may depend upon the why's and how's. A stereotypical evil dictator is brutal. He stays on top to maintain control, and to live and do as he pleases. Good parents also want to stay on top, but only to care for and reform the little, self-destructive revolutionaries they've birthed. Well-loved and well-trained, the usurpers often morph into good dictators with their own little revolutionaries in tow.

Life has given Eve no cause to believe that her creator is an evil dictator. Rather than simply doubt his hidden motivations, she should review what she knows of his behavior. He's the only source of good she's ever seen. Up to this point she's noticed nothing wrong with his creation. And he's no nervous twit, for his secret police don't intrude upon her life, not even upon this encounter with the serpent.

Even if Eve can't assess the potential value of becoming "like God," her inner self has already been fashioned to reflect divinity. Furthermore, she ought to understand that biting the hand which feeds her won't elevate her position. How could such an act turn her, a dependent creature, into a fully independent being, or even more unbelievable, into a self-existent creator-God? Following the serpent will only raise her little fist in defiance.

One might imagine that God, at worst, does everything simply to look good and receive praise, like emotionally needy parents who dish out gifts only for affirmation. There are, even today, theological assertions about God which amount to that. (We shouldn't be surprised. Theology was, is, and will be all over the map, and off its edges, too. Some theologians are even atheists.)

If the serpent opposes a selfish God, then he makes a telling point, though so far there is no evidence for his accusation. Instead, given what we know from the text thus far, the serpent seems more likely driven by envy and a desire for power. If so, his claims are psychological projection and empty hate speech at the highest level. We'll look at his words more closely now. Later, we'll watch how this ancient presidential election, with the serpent and the creator on the ballot, plays out.

... opened ... enlightened ...

We usually value knowledge, experience, and insight. We speak of open doors, the light of truth, and a bright future. But people who survive war, abuse, poverty, and loss often feel assaulted, not enlightened. Psychologists label post-traumatic stress a "disorder," not a blessing. Open eyes can see joy or horror. If Eve is tantalized by a mixture of good and bad, she may have at least a feeble excuse for her naivety. We do not.

... good and bad, right and wrong!

Whatever might be pure and lovely can be envisioned as polluted and broken. Why do we hanker for what can hurt? Many of us are fascinated by the "mysterious." That word comes from ancient Greek ideas about secret religions. While speaking of the Greeks, we should note a selection from their massive mythology. Pandora, "the receiver of all gifts," was the first woman. Curious about a certain jar, she opened it. The evil within escaped and invaded the world. We may possess a built-in curiosity, but we also know it killed the cat. Some things, and especially evil things, are better left unsought and unknown.

We seem to learn little that's really important. We often want to have it all, know it all, and be it all. Yet much which we seek brings sorrow. Soon after being elected president, Abraham Lincoln responded to his supporters, "Well, boys, your troubles are over now, but mine have just begun." The preacher of Ecclesiastes warns about our broken world: "The more we know, the more we grieve."[12] We may need knowledge about evil to rescue its victims. But better still if no rescue is required.

Whatever part of the serpent's earlier statements might be taken at face value, however slanderous or disturbing, his call to sample both good and evil is a big, flapping, red flag. We needn't jump off a building to learn the power of gravity. But, you might say,

---

12 See Ecclesiastes 1:18.

gravity isn't evil. So let's get closer to the point. We're not very bright if we choose suicide to experience death. It's time Eve exorcizes the serpent's spell on her ears. Otherwise, her eyes will be affected, too.

Chapter 4: Death

Then the woman noticed that the tree's fruit was, in fact, good for food. It looked luscious and like a fount of wisdom. So she took some and ate it. And she handed some to her husband, who was with her, and he also ate it. Then their eyes were opened. But what they saw was their nakedness. So they sewed fig leaves together, making coverings for themselves.[13]

What's the real you? Are you merely blood, bones, and brain cells, or are you something immaterial, something "spiritual"?

Before jumping back into the story, we'll explore this question from a philosophical approach. Many of you are already convinced that your personal existence goes beyond biology. And many people equate philosophy with tooth extraction. If both those things are true of you, feel free to skip this section. For the rest, souls like me who have been kicked around by such questions, the next part is important.

---

13 A note about this translation is found in the Appendix.

The Real Us

If, as a materialistic and so-called "scientific" approach to life asserts, you are your body and your body is you, then some disturbing truths become clear. Here are three.

- Your thoughts are generated by your body.
- You might be in a coma, imagining everything.
- When your body stops functioning, you will be gone forever.

But even as you read this sentence, you believe you're interacting with reality. You can't be in a coma. Instead, you see your body as a house for the real you, some kind of immaterial being. You receive sensory input, as if your body has doors and windows to the outside world. But you live inside. It is you, the occupant, not the house, who thinks, emotes, desires, and wills. Provable or not, it seems entirely reasonable that the inner you is real and distinct from your body. If that's right, a different set of profound truths become clear, entirely at odds with those above.

- The real you is not biological. It was not created by matter or from matter.
- Barring drugs, illness, or the like, your thoughts reflect the real you.
- When your body stops functioning, the real you might live on. Likewise, when the real you stops functioning, your body might live on.

Returning to our saga, we can draw some conclusions. If the serpent is right in saying Eve will not die, then eating the fruit will open her eyes to great wonders, and God will be exposed as a liar or fool. But if the serpent is wrong, then either Eve's body or her true self will die. The serpent will be exposed as a liar or fool, but it will be too late for Eve.

Those are the basics. We'll now see them play out, along with much more.

Then the woman noticed that the tree's fruit was, in fact, good for food. It looked luscious and like a fount of wisdom.

The creator put the tree right in the middle of the garden, not far off in some bramble-covered spot near the edge. The tree is central to his plans. In a sense, it still confronts us and stands more significant than education, marriage, or a career to young people venturing out on life. Like many of them, Eve hasn't looked closely at her future, and probably for good reason. Life is no doubt full with all its newness, and she's had little time to savor it. Other than her discussion with the serpent, the story presents no notable events which have intervened. Though the creature intrudes and awakens her attention, he points to what's already there. Sooner or later, Eve and her husband must each make a decision about the tree.

The fruit looks good. Actually, it looks very good, and even rewarding. We mustn't diminish that fact. Is it too good? Has the creator gone too far? Has he made a mistake? Has he set up an obstacle the first people simply cannot overcome? Or, God forbid, has he laid a trap?

Such scenarios should strike us as unlikely. The creator designed for his people a profoundly beautiful world in which, at least prior to the serpent's intrusion, everything was good. The fruit could not be otherwise, for the creator doesn't make junk. More important, a real choice requires a minimum of two good options. The tree's existence is no mere formality or a comforting rite of passage. It is the single crossroad on the way to vastly different destinations. The tree is there to be carefully considered.

What's more, we'd be wrong to blame the creator for making the fruit "too good." Why, we might ask, didn't he hang something else on the tree, like hideous, foul-smelling durians, or even just some large jackfruits? No. To claim that the fruit was "too good" is the equivalent of believing that the first humans, and we with them, are its defenseless victims. That would imply, even as we are often tempted to believe, that we're bound to do whatever seems natural or feels good. If we imagine Eve in such a spot, we condemn ourselves to her fate, slaves of our senses. We turn into leashed puppies, yanked about by the world around us. Self-coddling pity will ruin us. There are times when we need to use our own backbone, not cry on someone's shoulder.

So, the tree's fruit is essential to the creator's plan. But what's the plan? Given that he's shown no sign of being vicious, his purpose for the tree could lie anywhere along a continuum from test, to challenge, to opportunity. Whatever it may be, we have good reason to believe he wants the first people, and through them the rest of their world, to succeed.

But if the creator really wants success, why doesn't he show up and do something? Why doesn't he cheer them on, shout reminders, or even chide them into obedience? Two truths stand out in response. The first is a word we claim to love so much: freedom. But as we saw before, true freedom is both marvelous and dangerous. With it comes the right and the requirement to choose without obstruction or interference.

We may assume that the creator is merely watching the action from a heavenly armchair. Opposing that scenario is a second reason he doesn't appear in physical form. It harks back to our discussion about the mouth. As we often say, a great person is "as good as their word." The saga wants us to understand that in the garden, the creator's presence and what he says are one and the same.

God created by speaking.[14] Apparently, he wants to maintain things the same way, not so much by displays of power as by the unity of his heart (his own spirit, if you will) with his word. And so he encapsulates his presence in the command about

---

14 See Genesis chapter 1.

the tree. In that very tangible way he is, in fact, standing next to Eve, looking up with her at the great question of her life. What does she really want, her source or what it provides? The serpent, also standing nearby, has created nothing. But he does offer fabulous training in street tactics, like snatch and run. What will she do?

So she took some and ate it. And she handed some to her husband, who was with her, and he also ate it.

With these words, the saga calls us to pause and weep. Not merely for the first people, but for ourselves, others, and even for the creator.

We should reflect on Eve's recitation of the only law in paradise. Without cause or right, she added the phrase "or even touch it." Now, as she actually does touch the fruit, nothing happens. The absence of repercussions, substantiated by her inaccurate recitation, encourages her to keep going. And even immediately after eating, nothing happens. But the divine command never said that death would be instantaneous. If it had, Adam would have noticed a change in his wife. He would have grieved over her, but he would have survived.

Instead, the creator's gifts, used rightly or wrongly, come with time for enjoyment. But how long does the enjoyment last? Too long, it seems. For Eve again concludes there is no problem. The fruit tastes good, and she passes it on with pleasure.

As for Adam, the story says that he's right there "with her," just watching and waiting. So he's involved too, though in hollow form, diminished by his ambivalence.

What's to learn? Call it what you will, whether living life to the fullest, going for the gusto, enjoying what's at hand, disobedience, stupidity, or sin. Whatever it is, enjoyment comes to the two via the creator's work, however regrettable that enjoyment may prove to be.

Then their eyes were opened. But what they saw was their nakedness.

We could expound upon this at length, and easily too much for a short book. But we cannot overstate the significance of these few words.

As both the creator and the serpent predicted, the first human lives are radically altered. Adam and Eve now see what they've never noticed before. Not vast visions in the sky, or the path to a brilliant future, or the means to become more powerful beings. But they do indeed experience powerful forces, forces which will drive human history to its end: weakness, need, and shame. The couple has failed, they are exposed, and they are vulnerable.

Here, in a few simple words, the ancient saga claims to diagnose not only the condition of our ancestors, but that of their descendants. It tells us not only what they became, but who we are. Like the first man and woman, we too have failed, we are exposed, and we are vulnerable.

The inner self of the first people, each originally formed and cut like a divine jewel, lies shattered. Broken fragments remain. Their new life will be described and defined by what they do with the pieces.

Before we watch, a few observations conclude this scene.

Adam's greatest love becomes his demise. Romeo and Juliet go down together. But this is no tragic romance. In the final act, despite the serpent's role, neither of the lovers is the victim of injustice. Adam must either refuse Eve's offer of poisonous love, or die the fool at her side. Eve's beautiful form and outwardly gentle overture constitutes the world's first social pressure, and one of the most intense kind. The dearer our friends, the more difficult our choices. How very hard, and so very lonely, to do what is best.

Adam's situation is worse than Romeo's, but without pathos or excuse. His problem began earlier, when he simply watched Eve leap off a cliff. As the "firstborn," isn't it his role to warn, shout, or interfere? But he does nothing except chew and swallow. He leaves us a legacy as the first useless, beer guzzling, couch potato. That may seem harsh, but the next chapter enforces it.

What if, in the nick of time, Adam had risen from his stupor and dissuaded his lover from suicide? The serpent would not only be exposed, but shamed by lesser creatures who, rising to the challenge and passing the test, would thereby have advanced in experience and power. The tree's great purpose would then have been fulfilled. From there the creator might have challenged his people still further, each achievement making them more truly "like God." Alas.

If Adam had tried but failed to stop Eve, watching her demise would have been horrific. But the pain in paradise would pass, and the one who made the first woman could make a second.

We might divide the creator's world into two basic parts. First, there is the order of material things like heaven, earth, plants, animals, and human bodies. Second is the realm of spirits and their relationships. We could include among those relationships the man with himself alone, the man and his wife together, and each of them with their creator. The realm of such relationships is lofty. The order of material things is wonderful, but it is meant to serve. Associations of the spirit are the most rewarding. We might even imagine that a creature's relationship with the creator is the most delightful and wonderful of all. The tragedy of our story strikes us as both common and profound: the love of gifts usurps the giver.

The serpent's trick is now laid bare. He'd given Adam and Eve nothing, and couldn't care less about them. They were fodder for his larger goals. Like later revolutionaries without deep moral roots, his followers are expendable. They become simply his means to attack and supplant the enemy.

Ironically, the reward of the fruit was to be obtained not by eating it but by refusing it. To rise above the senses and reject the serpent is the way to become, in his own words, "like God, enlightened about good and bad, right and wrong." The tree's reward was to grant insight into the beauty of good and the ugliness of evil.

In a sense, the tree still stands today. But we don't tend to appreciate it. Healthy, happy self-love is not some suave, sensuous life animated by access to all the world's good things. Good is the enemy of the best. To let go of the first is to gain them both. A spring of water gives life after a glass of water is consumed.

So they sewed fig leaves together, making coverings for themselves.

Activity can be a wonderful healer, and repairs can improve lives. But by constructing a façade, the man and woman only make things worse. They exhibit and nurture a kind of insanity. How can the cause of soulish pain be addressed by covering the skin? How can our spiritual inside be fixed on the physical outside?

Granted, our couple is clever, a piece of the broken jewel which reflects their creator. As such they come up with what may be the first human inventions, the first cultural artifacts. They see a need. Then, they imagine the solution. From there they look for and find the right kind of materials. Then they devise the means to produce. Presto! They are creators too—united, smart, industrious, and productive! Even so, they are fools.

The serpent lied to them and tricked them. They now unconsciously imitate him, repeating his ruse upon themselves. They diminish the nature and complexity of their spiritual essence with a material fix.

A short while back they felt naked and vulnerable. Attempting to hide the situation from themselves and each other, they now imagine their shame is gone. They fancy themselves as self-sufficient, protected by their labors. They may even experience a new sensation: pride. In reality, everything points to their insurmountable problem. What their eating did was bad enough. Deluded by their useless remedy, they unwittingly feed their spiritual cancer.

And these things are only the first signs of Adam and Eve's death.

Chapter 5: Inquest

Later, during the cool time of day, they heard the Eternal God in the garden. So there among its trees the man and his wife hid themselves from him. But the Eternal God called out to the man, saying, "Where are you?"[15]

Our society may have dumped the Ten Commandments, but we've come up with a new list. *It's none of your business* is one of the favorites. The other nine, equally strong and assertive, say pretty much the same thing: *Private Property. Keep out. No Trespassing. Beware of Dog.*

We can be nasty neighbors. We'd do better to ask what authority has granted all this private property we fence off and defend. Legal-sounding justifications may appear strong. *It's my life! It's my right! Who are you to judge? That's hate!* They stand ready with a knockout punch. But a little bob and weave by a careful opponent turns the champion's jabs into shadow boxing. Return punches are more

---

15 A note about this translation is found in the Appendix.

likely to land. *Where'd you get that life of yours? Don't your choices affect others? If something's wrong, why not judge it? Shouldn't we love what's good and hate what's evil?*

A question also opens the inquest below. It's gentler than those above, but can eat like acid into steel.

Later, during the cool time of day, they heard the Eternal God in the garden.

Without doubt the creator is not pleased by what's happened. His first people have failed their only test. For a while, he occupies himself with whatever God does alone at home, giving them time to think. Only later does he descend to earth. He comes during the cool of the day, apparently a good time for walking and talking in the beautiful garden. He's not boiling over with oft-imagined Biblical wrath. He doesn't nuke the place or even burn it down. He simply shows up and, as it were, politely rings the doorbell.

So there among its trees the man and his wife hid themselves from him.

We can imagine their pathetic flight, like children crawling under beds. Life throws many dangers our way. We should avoid some and hide from others. But for the first couple to scurry away from their creator is another sign of the death he predicted.

First, they've become irrational. What can hide from the all-seeing eyes of the maker? Second, they unwittingly treat themselves with contempt. Their self-preservation becomes a kind of spiritual wrist cutting. For if there's any place to run, it should be in the opposite direction, toward life and a cure. Instead, they experience new sensations, much deeper and more powerful than those from the fruit in their mouths. Unable to stand and think clearly, they flee.

As if mirroring the truth of the saga, our language overflows with terms for such feelings: insecurity, weakness, shame, loss, futility, trepidation, guilt, disquiet, alarm, uncertainty, panic, nervousness, stress, anxiety, worry, apprehension, unease, angst, helplessness, torment, fright, confusion, exposure, unrest, tension, concern, premonition, terror, fretfulness, pressure, consternation, foreboding, doubt, horror, anguish, vulnerability, distress, grief, dread .... Or, as the man will later call it, fear.

The two are overcome. Instead of mental clarity and health, we watch death sink a large drill bit deep into their soul. If at the center of a human being lives a spirit, then here their spirits lie dying, unable to function properly. Neither medication nor counselors could fix it. When cut off from our source, we wither.

But the Eternal God called out to the man, saying, "Where are you?"

The divine voice speaks once more. In the beginning it created. With the fruit it commanded and challenged. Now it pursues. It doesn't curse or yell, but its words loom larger and more intrusive than the tree from which the people ate. Of course the creator knows where they are. Though cloaked, hiding, and comforted by each other's presence, whenever he arrives they are always visible. He offers them the chance to tell the truth. His voice reaches out, quite possibly in gentle tones. But we can't label his question nice or even polite, for by it the man first and then the woman are naked once more.

Some Other Questions

Granted, the saga here makes no direct claims about us. But later it does, so it's fair to assume that this scene, too, is more than a narrative. Watching the first people, we look in a mirror. It forces us to ponder and to think. The history of the human race is not pretty. Is there a cure? Who are we as individual members? What's the state of our own inner self? In what do we hope or hide?

The saga claims that we've all been infected. We may feel safe in our dens, whether physical or psychological, sensory or spiritual. But like Adam and Eve's clothing, and like the trees they crouch among, our efforts block reality only from ourselves. The serpent and the maker see it all very plainly. One laughs, the other grieves.

Chapter 6: Psychosis

"I heard you in the garden," the man replied. "Because I was naked, I became afraid and hid myself."

The Eternal God then asked, "Who told you that you are naked? Have you eaten from the tree which I forbade?"

The man replied, "The woman you put here with me, she gave me fruit from the tree. So I ate it."

Then the Eternal God turned to the woman, "What's this you have done?"

She said, "The serpent deceived me, and I ate."

Maybe you've seen people with psychosis. It's not a term to use lightly. Webster's gives a basic definition:

- A mental disorder characterized by symptoms, such as delusions or hallucinations, that indicate impaired contact with reality.

- Any severe form of mental disorder, as schizophrenia or paranoia.

In those dictionary terms, the first people's responses, especially Adam's, "indicate" a sudden and dramatic "impaired contact with reality." As for Eve, an entertainer years ago adopted her "paranoia" as his theme: "The devil made me do it!" But in the garden, no one's laughing. Are their answers calculated to deceive? If so, only someone with "delusions or hallucinations" could imagine God being impressed.

Probably the words simply fly out of their mouths, like the contents of an unhappy stomach. Even so, we find it easy to sympathize with our forebears. We see them as quite sane, not unlike ourselves. What's more, there's clearly some truth in what they say.

Silly us. There's some truth in almost everything. With the exception of a bare "Yes" or "No," truth is the basis for every lie and reality for every mirage.

And after a bit of sympathy, we notice things about the first people which make us cringe. This is a great story, and the details of the ancient mess deserve close scrutiny. On their own, some are quite funny. Maybe they're even intended that way to help us laugh at ourselves.

"I heard you in the garden," the man replied. "Because I was naked, I became afraid and hid myself."

The Eternal God then asked, "Who told you that you are naked? Have you eaten from the tree which I forbade?"

The man replied, "The woman you put here with me, she gave me fruit from the tree. So I ate it."

Adam explains his behavior in chronological order. It's all so very reasonable. He was naked, he felt fear, and he hid. But he's irrational. Up to this point he'd never known fear. He'd been with the creator before. Only this time does his presence feel dangerous. Furthermore, Adam was clothed, but he claims to be naked. His efforts at covering up, seemingly helpful at first, are useless in the presence of God.

Adam is having a focus problem. Let's put some words in his mouth and move things closer to the truth.

> *I did something. Afraid of you, I tried to hide.*

The inquest continues.

> *Adam, did you eat the fruit?*

His answers go from bad to worse. This story is deadly serious, but Adam plays the perfect stooge. Somber analysis and heavy theology will miss the point. So here's some hopefully helpful fun. It makes explicit what Adam hopes is read between the lines.

> *Dear Sir, I trust you to hear my defense, for what I have to say is truly how things stand. Excuse me for being*

so blunt, but you are the one who started this problem. It was you who made this woman and put her here. You probably meant well, but you must admit that I never imagined such a being. I didn't ask for her and couldn't do anything but accept her. That's fact number one. Second, it was she who handed the fruit to me. I didn't take it from the tree, and would never willingly disobey your command. I'm better than that. These two truths are indisputable, and more than sufficient to exonerate me. But if I may, the truth doesn't stop there. Frankly, she's not like a man. She won't take no for an answer. Yes, I ate some of the fruit, but if I hadn't, I'd never enjoy a moment's peace. She gave me no choice. In summary, I declare my innocence. And if I may say, Sir, please consult with me before any further unelected surgeries on my ribs. The defense rests.

If Adam is anything, he's a believer in himself. His first court appearance is stunningly bold. Never mind that he simply watched Eve walk off a cliff. Never mind that he followed right after. Never mind that he turned coward and traitor against his once-cherished wife. Never mind that he blamed it all on his generous maker.

Adam's excuses engulf the truth like pea soup fog. Because of it, we may even have trouble seeing things clearly ourselves. A simple one-word response to the "Have you eaten?" would be sufficient and true: "Yes." The first man, made to reflect divinity, is stripped and guilty. Instead of bowing his head to seek mercy, he rises with pride. He attacks others, defends himself, destroys whatever integrity he might salvage, and becomes a political cartoon for the ages. Hypocrisy runs strong and deep in the human soul. It's both hilarious and very sad.

Then the Eternal God turned to the woman, "What's this you have done?"

She said, "The serpent deceived me, and I ate."

"Deceive" is a word we tend to reserve for the innocent. To deceive a crook is delicious irony, the stuff of books and movies. Is Eve innocent? The serpent presented bold-face lies. Eve knew and spoke the truth, but she chose to replace it with self-gratification. So she wasn't simply deceived.

Her choice damaged her own future, and by that means she compromised the future of her husband. And then she kept going, in effect asking him to die with her. She doesn't mention any of that here. Nevertheless, Eve comes out a bit better than Adam. He blamed the good guy. At least she blamed the bad guy. But she still can't come to grips with the truth. The serpent didn't force her to do anything.

Their blame-shifting only belittles themselves and enslaves them to others. By dismissing their guilt, they add to it. After hearing lies, they also lie. The world's first love story becomes a tragic farce. The sad ironies just keep piling up. The serpent is in stitches.

But, we may say, "It was just a little bite of fruit! It's small stuff! There's so much that's far worse!"

Like almost anything, there's some truth in that too. But is it true? Look again at what happened to the first people after their "little bite." They both distorted the facts. Adam tried to shift blame and punishment to his wife, making him the first coward, wife-abuser, and hater. He even had the arrogance to slander his maker. Imagine doing that to your boss at work. One decision and a little snow off the mountain top becomes an avalanche. Truth is indivisible. To reject part is to reject it all, turn one's back away from home, and wander into the wilderness. We don't dismiss a headache by saying "It's just a little brain cancer."

Furthermore, the first people's choices affect others, too. They unleash a virus upon humanity. Later, things get even uglier. Their first child hates his innocent brother and kills him. As a reflection of his parents, the killer defies the judge.[16]

The saga asks us to ponder how and where we also hide. What we take pride in and consider success might well be delusion, fig leaves, and a forest covering our inner brokenness. The saga also tells us to mourn. To the extent we bemoan the state of the world we understand its psychosis.

This is all very deep water, and it's hard to know what's worse, saying too little or too much. A good way to end might be a few aphorisms, some tongue-in-cheek, which summarize the key truths.

---

16 See Genesis 4:1, ff.

The world is full of liars, and the one we should fear the most is in the mirror.
Rationality thinks it rules, but the senses drug it and the ego tricks it.
Lies which hurt are very ugly; those which help seem so lovely.
The best friend of wounded pride is blame-shifting.
To acquire and strut proves what to whom?
Spiritual health is known by its company.
To seek respect is to betray its lack.

Chapter 7: Hostility

The Eternal God then addressed the serpent, "Because you did this, of all animals, domestic or wild, you are the most cursed. You will creep on your belly, licking dust every day of your life. And I will make you and the woman enemies, likewise your offspring and hers. Her offspring will strike your head, and you will strike her offspring's heel."[17]

It's evil to hurt the innocent. Hurting them for pleasure is worse. Likewise, some actions are evil, but truly wicked people are outrageous. Our most popular movies don't fight evil in the abstract. That's boring. We want to look at a face and see it run over by justice.

But as we consider history or simply read the daily news, we often sense that evil people live in the shadow of something larger. The more despicable they are, the more it seems that other forces are also

---

17 A note about this translation is found in the Appendix and later in this chapter.

involved. Mankind's worst horrors almost demand the existence of something beyond us, something out there which is truly diabolical. And what greater source of evil than a treacherous, alien power hiding among us?

Our saga is a spine-chiller. We see here a monstrous enemy who hates everything the creator makes, from insects to sunsets. But his favorite hunting ground is among humans, the foolish, weak, yet beloved focus of his great enemy. And among those weak creatures, he especially hates "the woman" and "her offspring," those who are given the infuriating, divine ability to advance the species.

War has begun.

The Eternal God then addressed the serpent, "Because you did this, of all animals, domestic or wild, you are the most cursed. You will creep on your belly, licking dust every day of your life.

In the now damaged world, all life suffers, plants, animals and their caretakers together. But one creature is cursed above all. The creator is not talking here about snakes. They're but a reminder of something more powerful and insidious. The evil being which invaded earth is condemned to exile among those he tried to destroy. He forfeited his earlier home with the Great Spirit beyond. The inferior beings populating this lower sphere were made from the dirt which blows in his filthy mouth, a constant reminder of his cursed, belittled existence.

The serpent chose to oppose the creator. The first people foolishly followed. They now regret that choice. The once big talker has nothing to say before the bigger judge. A supernatural conflict will be fought in this dusty place, and each side will endure its fate.

And I will make you and the woman enemies, likewise your offspring and hers. Her offspring will strike your head, and you will strike her offspring's heel."

A supposedly good God fosters a sprawling war? How can this be? The serpent moved first. The creator's people then opened the door. War may be hell, but there's little choice: fight or be annihilated, accept the call or curl up and be destroyed. Yet the woman and her kind, if now a bit wiser, stand ill-equipped against their foe. The creator's prophesy seems laughable. Without his help, people are doomed.

The creator will strengthen the woman and allow her to give birth. Her offspring will become a great force. The serpent, too, will have his own "offspring," probably at least other spirits drawn to his side. From this point on he will not just talk. He will attack. But though wounded, the woman's offspring will somehow thwart his plans.

The prophecy is expansive but gives few details. Adding to the mystery is the way it's stated. The wording of the Hebrew original is vague, no doubt intentionally so. The issues have been debated for millennia, and the ambiguity is reflected in English translations. The quotation that follows comes from the Appendix, where the translation done for this book is presented. The discussion is important but technical. Skip it if you must and start up again with the summary immediately after.

The Hebrew nouns and their possessive suffixes [...] are most simply translated "your offspring/seed" and "her offspring/seed," singular in form but potentially plural in meaning. Also singular are the Hebrew pronouns in the second sentence, which might be more literally translated, "He will strike your head, and you will strike his heel." Translations done by Christians more often than not retain the grammatical singular form "he/his," whereas Jewish understanding tends toward the plural "they/their." The translation here has purposely slithered in between, using the somewhat tiresome repetition of "her offspring" in lieu of a singular or plural pronoun. Though the theological implications are potentially large either way, they are not dependent upon the grammatical number of the Hebrew or upon this verse alone. Furthermore, as is not uncommon in prophetic passages like this, the goal could be to encompass at least two different meanings to be fulfilled in distinct ways.

In summary, the meaning and future of the woman's "offspring" may lead us in two different directions. But we shouldn't be surprised. Divine predictions are sometimes intended to do just that. The creator, it seems, is saying two things at once: 1) The woman and her descendants will constantly be at war with the serpent and his forces; 2) A particular descendant of the woman will ultimately destroy the serpent and undo his work.[18]

Some Related Thoughts

A careful look at the inquest reveals five parts. The creator begins with Adam, moves to Eve, addresses the serpent, returns to Eve, and ends with Adam. The study of literature refers to this device as a chiasm. The central item is usually in focus. Here, that would be the serpent, consistent with it being first "on stage." Chapters 1 and 2 of Genesis tell the story of creation, and they begin with the creator. Our saga, chapter 3, is the story of destruction, and it begins with the serpent. Even so, the creator has the last word.

The saga calls the serpent a misogynist and misopedist, a hater of women and their offspring. Some of us may see it all as far-fetched, or even a collection of fantasy and illusion. On the other hand, if we compare this to the world as we know it, we have reason to think again. Highly disturbing conditions confront women, troubles which are less known or entirely unknown among men.

For example, whatever we may believe about today's rampant pornography, more often than not women are at the center. Can we possibly maintain that it's

18 Excluded from our discussion is the simplistic interpretation that women in general will fear snakes.

meant to honor them? Do lofty ideals drive this multi-billion dollar international industry? No. It degrades the female gender to the level of an object and a toy. Women lose.

Likewise, whatever we may believe about the legality and legitimacy of abortion—and here women stand entirely alone—no woman strives to get pregnant only to enjoy the thrill of an abortion. Whether we consider it murder, a necessary evil, or mere surgery, it's hardly something to celebrate. And whether or not our considerations include what's aborted, whether we view it as human life or mere tissue, worldwide statistics say that over half of what's eliminated, if given the chance, would become a woman. Women lose again.

Furthermore, we cannot ignore the historical and still widespread second-class status of women around the world, whether at the level of nations, cultures, economies, or families. (We're not talking here primarily about wealthy democracies, relatively recent in human history and by no means the vast majority of nations today. Though even there, we could.) And beyond the already noted pornography is face-to-face sexual use and abuse, some on an international scale. None of this is an honor to either gender. But once more, women lose most.

When considering the story, might the worldwide menace against women, both ancient and modern, be more than simple happenstance?

Finally, while consumed by these painful issues, we may miss an obvious lesson. We are all born of a woman. It's impossible to say to what extent history's murder and mayhem is purely human as opposed to something more. But so much appalls us that it's hard to discount that "something more." As descendants of Eve, maybe the serpent strikes us all. We each interpret and understand these things as we will. But our many thoughts and discussions aside, we cannot avoid our many losses. We all lose. We have all lost.

With the instigator now condemned, we move on to the creator's prophesies about his people. They speak of more pain, but also of life and hope.

Chapter 8: Consequences

To the woman he said, "I will make childbearing very painful for you, and in pain you will give birth. You will want your husband, but he will rule over you."

And to Adam he said, "You did what your wife said—you ate from the tree which I forbade. Because of you, the land is now cursed. In pain you will survive on it all the days of your life. It will give you thorns and thistles, and you'll eat what grows in its fields. Your food will come by the sweat of your brow, until you return to the land from which you were made. For you are but dust, and to dust you will return."[19]

Generalities and Gender

Generalities are limited but necessary. The key is to generalize rightly and remember there will be exceptions. Not all kinds of birds fly (e.g., ostriches, penguins, or extinct dodos). Neither can baby birds, nor those with a broken wing. But saying "birds fly"

---

19 A note about this translation is found in the Appendix.

is still true and helpful. Some squirrels are said to fly, though more properly they simply glide. And some rodent-like mammals, not related to birds, fly incredibly well. We call them bats. On the other hand, cats don't fly, nor do oysters, though if you throw an oyster, you might say it flew. You might also force a little kitten to fly off a tall building, but hopefully you won't.

We don't argue about most generalizations. But we certainly do when it comes to the nature of men and women. We make and change laws about it, debate issues, and march in the streets. Besides obvious physical differences, the mere fact that we use two words, *man* and *woman*, shows that we believe in both certain distinctions and generalities.

The Battle of the Sexes?

The saga boldly predicts the gender divide and makes sweeping claims about it. We may note exceptions, but that proves little. Some oppose the claims, but they're forced to replace them with others. To deny the differences between the sexes is to blind ourselves.

Here's an attempt at an itemized summary of the saga's claims and their implications. (We'll discuss the man's "rule" a bit later.)

- The natural state of a woman is to want a man.
- Likewise, a man needs a woman, as the creator himself said.[20]

---

20 See Genesis 2:18.

- Their focus differs: women tend toward propagation, men toward preservation and protection.
- Each is vital, like one leg to the other. Individuals can survive and even prosper with only one leg, but that requires special skills.
- Children not only derive from and reflect their parents, they ultimately derive from the creator and reflect him.

If the author of our ancient story were alive today, before he published such claims we might expect him to consult with his readers, or carry out an extensive survey, or allow for a vote. But his story asserts that the relationship between the sexes is more a matter of reality than opinion. If so, can it be subjected to a vote?

We may, of course, vote regardless. But we must also live. And as we live, we should note how others have lived before us. It's no small thing to see the saga's claims about men and women reflected in the annals of history, if not always in changing human opinions.

Shouldn't those who believe they have better ideas for our species test them thoroughly? Given our long history, would social experiments spanning a mere two or three hundred years be too much to expect? In fact, that kind of time frame would seem to be essential for determining the effects on succeeding generations. To be valid, such experiments should include a large, mixed-age populace. Ethically speaking, the participants must be entirely willing. Finally, consistent with good science, the experimental sample must be isolated so as not to affect or be affected by the rest of us. Barring all this, is it too much to ask that those who dream of different realities limit their experiments to their own precious lives?

We return to children and work. The saga claims that both were designed as part of the original, perfect order. But now things don't function properly, each pursuit becomes far more difficult, and new issues intrude. Of course, women work too, with or without children. And men help, or should, with the children. And there are no babies without men (or at least not without their genes). But the basic generalities continue, and they provide us a framework and perspective for life. Even if we ignore or reject them, we tend to live them out in practice.

Death, the final part of the prophecy above, comes inexorably, and in the end without any fuzzy borders. After birth, it looms as the most unavoidable, overriding fact of our existence. An artist's imaginary lineup of bent, ape-like creatures may depict a vibrant, vertical man at the summit. But our real-life experience is far different. We move downhill. All humanity reflects and endures the prophetic curse. If we escape it until middle age, we begin to demonstrate the artist's lineup in reverse order, descending from healthy, upright adults to older, weaker creatures, ever more bent. Finally, we go down still further, into the earth.

Women's efforts with children keep the species from the demise of our dodo bird. Men's efforts help the women and children survive, so that the latter also give birth. But all bodies return to the biological source. As we often say at funerals, *Ashes to ashes, dust to dust.*

Childbirth

Here's another aspect of the prophecy we observe in nature. Birth in the animal world seems to be relatively easy. Most bacteria divide, an internally amazing but outwardly simple process. Fish are fine after spawning. And even with salmon, it's not their spawning which kills them. No doubt some female deer die while calving. But more often than not they give birth and immediately get on with life. Why don't women? No matter how healthy, active, or "close to nature" they may be, one of the greatest events in their life typically involves extreme effort, pain, and a significant degree of danger. Only then, hopefully, is it followed by joy.

Work and Death

Few people are born into an easy life. Most of us must sweat to survive. Even those handed bags of gold at birth must pay a price. If they don't sweat, the money they trust to make them a comfortable somebody will likely twist them into a self-centered nobody. Yet either way, our time is short. All of us go down in a matter of decades. The decline begins well before the end, the pain grows, and the process is permanent. Our life may not, in Hobbes' famous words, be "solitary, poor, nasty, [and] brutish." But neither can we stop it from ending.

And not only us. Everything grows "thorns and thistles." However we may try to forget that unceasingly nettlesome fact, we cannot seem to strike the infamous second law of thermodynamics from our world. How, amidst the incredible creation surrounding us, did this destruction come into play? And it rules not only over our bodies, but also over our food, houses, means of transportation, defenses, and the things we make to entertain us. It even rules over the grander wonders of nature. The sun will one day burn itself out. Then our beloved blue and green planet, like our own bodies, will also return to dust.

We scream "No!" We struggle and sweat, in part because we have to, and in part because we want to. Work is hard, but it's good, too. The story claims that, like our creator, activity gives us meaning and significance. We exist, at least in part, so that we might do. The ability to conceive, plan, strive, and give birth, birth to things both physical and biological, are some of the creator's good gifts to us. Despite our pressing problems, when absorbed in these good things we reflect our spiritual source.

The Hard Part?

As with almost anything, getting the context right is vital. Imagine being bound to long ropes. It sounds terrible. But what if you're falling from the sky? And what if, at the other end of your ropes, a parachute spreads out above? In that case your bonds are a life-saver.

It's something like that with men and women. Our story's statement, "… he will rule over you," sounds very restrictive. Ignorant men have often used it that way. They lift it up for all to see, as if it's their divine right to dominate, exploit, and belittle women. They proceed to oppress them, use them, and trash them. Such men are not only destructive but (excuse the plain English) stupid. The context of our story says something very, very different. Yes, it speaks, as it were, of ropes and rulers, but of ropes which save and rulers who protect.

Adam and Eve experienced a spiritual death. Only later will they physically die. In the meantime, the creator begins an astounding turnaround. Eve, the one to first dance with death, becomes the source of ongoing life. Her offspring will even defeat the serpent. How can it be?!

Adam, for his part, must provide. What's more, he must also protect, for very soon humanity will descend into violent chaos. The couple's firstborn son will kill his younger brother. The blood has flowed ever since.[21]

Our story is chock full of ironies. Eve, the first to choose death, becomes the source of life. She is the propagator. Adam, having abandoned his

_____
21 See Genesis 4:1-24.

God-given calling, sank with her. He must now rise to his responsibilities. The self-appointed leader must cede her position. The new ruler is not in place to dominate, but to provide and protect. Food, shelter, and defense will become essential but elusive. The man, the woman, and their future children are driven out into a difficult and deadly world.

Returning to the rope analogy, we might envision the first two people falling off a high cliff. The man is like a parachute. Of necessity, the woman is bound to him. Of necessity, he is also bound to her. It's absurd to say that the man is superior, for without her there will be no life, and nothing to save. Likewise, she cannot survive without his efforts. Only together will they find their purpose, meaning, and salvation.

Adam's "rule" over his wife is as much a sign of the cursed earth as his eventual death. The creator originally oversaw a reign of goodness and uncountable blessings. For their part, reflecting him, men and women were to rule over their domain together.[22] Now Adam must take over the mess he and his wife have created. Only a fool would say "lucky me!" Wise men will step up with humility, remembering to cherish and honor women. Wise women will show respect and appreciation. The one is not to coerce, and the other need not cower. Together they will fight the cursed conditions and the cursed serpent that instigated it all.

---

22 See Genesis 1:26-28.

The saga continues to expand. This is just the start of the relationship between the sexes, the beginning of struggles all around, and the onset of the battle against evil. Much more is revealed and discussed elsewhere. But everything begins here.

So we say that women (and to a lesser extent men) propagate and nurture. Men (and to a lesser extent women) provide and protect. And birds (mostly) fly.

Some Concluding Thoughts

We have already mentioned funerals. Two sentences prior to Adam and Eve meeting the serpent, their story is prefaced by lines often quoted at weddings. We find them here in an old but familiar form: "Therefore shall a man leave his father and his mother, and shall cleave unto his wife: and they shall be one flesh."[23]

Immediately after the garden disaster, our story proclaims the nuclear family: man, woman, and children. As such, the family is restored and remains to this day the basic social unit of human existence. Everything else, whether it be a village, clan, tribe, race, nationality, government, institution, or international body, though not unimportant, stands on the shoulders of the family.

But like anything in this now broken world, family is not without its own difficulties and dangers. As we saw in the story, the creator's best gift to Adam is what tempted him to leave the creator. Adam failed

23 From *The King James Version* of Genesis 2:24.

of his own accord but placed blame on the gift. And to this day many of his male heirs continue to blame woman for their problems. Women often return the honor.

Entire theological philosophies are built to keep women at bay and suppressed. And what better way to do so than by claiming divine support, however imaginary? Newer philosophies try the reverse and make men the scapegoat. Celibate monks and priests of diverse and even antithetical faiths around the world may seem to avoid many of the issues entirely. Sadly, their admirable efforts at self-suppression sometimes result in still larger problems for themselves and others.

Can't we view all these gender issues from a more hopeful perspective? Wouldn't we do better to see the two sexes as a wonderful gift from the creator? Despite our head-scratching and teeth-grinding, the relationship between man and woman can also be a wonderful source of mutual growth and respect. Like fire in a hearth, it welcomes both family and guests, cooks our food, and drives away the ever-encroaching cold. But when the fire is neglected, it will die out, or even burn the place down.

Chapter 9: Hope

Then the man named his wife Eve, for she would be the mother of all human life.

And the Eternal God made for Adam and his wife garments of skin and clothed them.

Our story began with an intrusion. The serpent walked on stage, demanded attention, and stirred up a typhoon. The storm is now over. For the present, the beast has retreated. The scene is short. It uses no big words. The first and best relationships, those between Adam, Eve, and their creator, are restored. Hope returns.

The waters seem calm, but their depths reach down beyond our ability to plumb.

Then the man named his wife Eve, for she would be the mother of all human life.

What are we to make of these few, choice words?

Earlier, Adam had jumped off a cliff. He'd walked up to the edge, looked over, and leapt. He made his choice. He'd been given real rights, and it was nobody's job to stop him from exercising them.

As predicted, Adam "died" spiritually. He's now been tried and held responsible. One day he will die physically, too. Until then, troubles will pursue him. But out of kindness and love, he's been granted another chance on earth.

And he will become a father after all. The woman he'd blamed is once again his precious one, "the mother of all human life." Though Adam will not live to see it, her offspring will finally defeat the enemy. Adam's faith in the future stands stronger than before. He has even more reason to trust the creator's promises for good. Through them he has hope, that basic necessity of life. Adam is flying over the moon with joy. Reflection, regret, relief. You might say he's reborn.

And the Eternal God made for Adam and his wife garments of skin and clothed them.

Weather conditions aside, much could be said about the fact that we still cover ourselves in public. Why? Nakedness shocks us. We gape at it, grimace, or laugh. We've built vast industries to record and sell it. We call their product pornography. The word's two root forms mean to document prostitution. Which only prompts us to ask again, what's going on?

We are very strange creatures. Our odd fixations regarding clothing betray deeper, spiritual problems. Though some animals may at times seem frustrated or confused by external circumstances, the story claims that we humans are disordered from within. We weren't designed that way, but now things are out of whack. We noted some of the symptoms earlier.[24] Here, the creator addresses them with deeply symbolic actions.

By clothing Adam and Eve, he reminds them of their past and gives them hope for the future. But that act requires an immense change.

Prior to the storm in their lives, the creator was largely quiet, unobtrusive, and gentle. He spoke mostly through his art. He was the source of beauty and wonder, the inventor of light and color, of living greenery, of sky and water. He filled the earth with animals of all kinds. They are tiny, massive, lively, lumbering, clever, dense, colorful, camouflaged, playful, serious, hilarious, graceful, and beautiful. He gave the first couple eyes, ears, a nose, and taste buds to appreciate it all, even sexual pleasure for them to experience one another and to express their love. Quite simply, he lavished his people with delight. Now, he opens a butcher shop.

There's no sense that the couple had ever even seen a dead animal. There's certainly no mention that they ate one, or that animals ate one another.[25]

---

24 See chapter four.
25 See Genesis 1:29-30.

Vegetarians, take heart. Now the two find themselves covered with bloody skins. The once gentle, playful artist has created a shocking, ghastly, and horrifying piece of work. Whatever for? What does it all mean?

First, a little diversion.

Some History

The Bible is a long book, and it carries on from here through many pages covering many centuries. Dead animals became central to its religious rites. Though most were ultimately consumed as food, the sacrificial process served as a sobering, no doubt often bleating, bellowing, and always bloody testimony to human spiritual need. It was intended to do just that.

However, blood is hardly restricted to the ancient Hebrew temple system. In fact, that system ended nearly 2000 years ago when Roman legions destroyed the last Jewish temple. Truly, the concept of sacrifice is far from limited to the Jews. The death of living ransoms, in one form or another, has been central to almost every culture. Even in our so-called modern world, the crimson liquid of life still flows. Once a year faithful Muslims, a significant percentage of earth's population, sacrifice animals.

The blood, however, hasn't always been from animals. History and archeology tell us that spanning the globe are sites, monuments, temples, and tombs where humans were sacrificed.

And if not animals or humans, religious offerings in more pleasant forms abounded, as they do today: candles, incense, food, drink, flowers, and the like. And even when not to gods or departed spirits, a kind of sacrifice is still central in the secular sphere, often simply as donations to this cause or that need. Governments encourage the practice, and even enshrine the offerings in tax law.

Why do we sacrifice, if not for deeply felt, even unconscious spiritual reasons? A materialistic world where the fittest survive rejects such demands. We might, sometimes, give to truly help others. But don't we almost always do it to feel good about ourselves, or at least a bit better? In reality, we don't live in a materialistic world. Our world is spiritual, and matter is its mask. To have peace, the human soul requires sacrifice.

The Message

We now return to the story. The creator himself is grieved. His plans appear to be in tatters. Yet he remains the gentleman. He doesn't hate. He doesn't scream or shout. He doesn't berate them, hit them, fence them in or lock them up. Instead, the first couple is ushered, as it were, into the world's first slaughterhouse. They are to observe and to learn.

The creator understands their sense of spiritual need. He acknowledges their desire to deal with it, but he must reject their own efforts as insufficient. The damage the two caused is far more extensive than their ability to restore. Fig leaves just won't do.

In effect, they had handed their lives and their world over to the serpent. They possess nothing to offer in restitution. Only new life can replace its loss, and only the creator can provide that. Death was not the original plan. Now, something even more frightful, the life of the innocent, is somehow necessary. Beautiful creatures lay skinned and dead.

Though Adam and Eve may have never seen a dead animal, they must live with its outward form wrapped around them. Their initial attempts at clothing, a symbol of their desire to create and restore, are replaced by a constant reminder of their original failure. Like bright prison garb, their clothing displays their past. The skins declare its wearers to be convicts. They killed themselves, their relationships, the creator's plans for them, and now, in effect, their own pets. The brutality brings severe shame. But it also brings deep relief, for they are clothed with a profound and mysterious forgiveness.

Loose Ends

We conclude by noting some loose ends.

Two unanswered questions about this part of the story are particularly important. First, is the death of animals really sufficient to restore a person, or is it simply a symbol of something more profound? Second, how might the creator's taking of life in order to restore it relate to his promise that Eve's offspring will defeat the serpent? Along with that, we might ponder something else. Could the two answers be related, and if so, how?

The story will soon close on a somber note. But it leaves us with hope. And these two questions imply another hope—that we, the readers, will seek answers.

Chapter 10: Exile

Then he said, "The man has now become like one of us, with experience of right and wrong. He must not be allowed to also take and eat fruit from the tree of life, for then he would live forever!" So the Eternal God banished the man from the Garden of Eden to till the land from which he had been made. After driving the man out, at the entrance of the Garden of Eden he stationed angelic guards and a flaming, flashing sword to block the way to the tree of life.

The story ends where our own stories begin. Life is not as we would have it. War has forced everyone from paradise. The perfect garden is forever closed. Death is the only exit from the refugee camps, the only passport out of exile.

Human history and our individual part in it can bring short-term success. But everything ends in frustration. Like King Sisyphus of ancient mythology, we roll a rock up a great hill of trouble. Sooner or later, our achievements are limited. The hill is higher than we think, and the rock always rolls back down.

Might the creator have foreseen our fate and provided a solution? By him forgiving the first couple and promising the serpent's defeat, we have reason to hope that another paradise awaits. But it will not be here, on our beloved, bedeviled earth.

Any new garden will come from the maker of the old. Next time, the developer will live on the premises. No one will be forced to stay, and revolution will be unthinkable. Life won't be a matter of rules, but of reality. The people will have learned that anarchy doesn't work. There's only one being equipped to make good gardens, and neither he, nor his future occupants, will allow for another disaster.

Until then, we must deal with a creator who may seem dead set against us ....

Then he said, "The man has now become like one of us, with experience of right and wrong. He must not be allowed to also take and eat fruit from the tree of life, for then he would live forever!"

We don't like those words, "not allowed." Yet we can't live without them. We make rules for children, students, parents, doctors, policemen, drivers, pilots, seamen, teachers, business people, armies, and politicians. Even street gangs and drug cartels have their own rules. Rules, rules, rules!

But the creator himself was never gaga over any of that. At the beginning, he gave just one negative rule about one tree. Everything else was basically: "Wonderful place to live! Enjoy!"

Due to our now malfunctioning surroundings and dysfunctional selves, more and more rules rain down upon us. We humans have made the vast majority. We've enshrined them as legislation, laws, injunctions, rulings, edicts, decrees, sanctions, orders, regulations, proclamations, taboos, bans, socially unacceptable behavior, and on and on. Attempting to order our messy world, we institute far more restrictions than the creator ever did.

Now, as the story winds down, we hear that another tree, mentioned earlier,[26] can give unending life. But at precisely the time of the first people's greatest need, the creator blocks their way to it. What's with that? Isn't this deadly restriction, enforced by invincible policemen, proof that the creator simmers with anger? Has he soured on us? Is he unforgiving, nasty, or even malicious?

Another Tree and Other Beings

The answers come to us masterfully nuanced. The rationale behind this second negative decree is a bit complicated, and we'll try to keep details to a minimum. Patience will yield its fruit, for after we navigate the issues, more of the saga's grand vistas will emerge.

---

26 See Genesis 2:9.

To view the scenery, we must understand three puzzling bits of the divine rationale: "the man," "one of us," and "experience of right and wrong." So-called professionals and readers of all types have given numerous interpretations. But extensive learning isn't required. The immediate context is our best friend, far more faithful than terms and theologies gathered from elsewhere.

First, "the man" means Adam, as it did earlier. But now he is not alone. The woman, source of his offspring, is clearly going with him out of the garden. So at this point, the term stands for both, and therefore ultimately for mankind.

Next, to determine who might be included in the phrase "one of us," we need to back up a bit. When the time had come to introduce humans into the world, creator said, "Let us make...." It was he who formed the man and the woman, and he alone. There was just one creator. No one else is mentioned.[27] So, contrary to what some people think, when God said "Let us make," he wasn't asking for help from an up-to-that-point unnamed audience of spirit beings, nor was he patronizing them while they merely watched. The creator's first "us" refers to him alone. He is introduced as a mysterious, majestic plurality, one that exists in, of, and by himself.

Later, which for us is our present place in the story, the creator says something different: "The man has

_____

27 See Genesis chapters 1 and 2 in general, and 1:26, 27 in particular.

become like one of us." If the creator were the only spiritual being around, why not just say "like us" as he had before? Something else is afoot. Or better, someone else is afoot.

The clue lies in tracking this carefully crafted story. Only after the creator made the world does the serpent step on its stage. And now we see still other beings. After the creator evicts the people from the garden, he posts angelic guards at its entrance. So at this point, well after the creation, we see that the creator is not alone in his spiritual realm. His more expansive "one of us" refers to any of three supernatural beings: the creator, the serpent, and the angelic guards. There may be others in view as well.

So let's summarize. The saga begins with a creator. He made people. We then learn of other beings. Given his power and supremacy, their various responses to him, and the entire context, they were also made by him, though we are not told when. Some of those beings have chosen to stay with their creator. Others will not.

Put another way, in the unseen word, there are good spirits, bad spirits, and a supreme spirit. There may even be many kinds of good and bad spirits. Who knows all they are up to? Throughout the world native peoples practice "indigenous religions." I have lived among some. Their beliefs often align directly with this scenario. Like our saga, they also claim that nature is infused with the spiritual, a kind of matter and antimatter. What we see is only the façade.

As for the third and final bit of the creator's statement, namely "with experience of right and wrong," we earlier discussed the serpent's very similar words, "enlightened about good and bad, right and wrong." We saw how enlightenment comes in more than one way. We all know, for example, about suicide, but none of us has successfully done it. And we've all heard of people who choose a life of crime. But hopefully we won't do the same. Many things are better known only theoretically, potentially, and from afar. Adam and Eve chose the oft-vaunted "experiential" route to enlightenment, and now they regret it. Sadly, many of their descendants will not just make bad choices, they will love them. Welcome to life as we know it.

So we might expand and rephrase the translation above like this:

> We have a problem, and I, as the supreme being, must deal with it. Sadly, humans have become like us, we who, forever divided, inhabit the world of spirits. Now, with first-hand experience of both right and wrong, some people will long for what is good, but others, what is evil.

A Final Question

But, we might ask, if the understanding above is correct, why would the creator want to stop both types of people from living forever? Shouldn't they each receive a different fate?

The answer, once again, is both weighty and simple. Those who cherish good should not be stuck forever in this damaged place. Those who cherish evil should not be allowed to forever enjoy it. Love for the first group and justice for the second demand that each come to an end. After that, our saga gives good reason to hope that those who want something better will find it.

So the Eternal God banished the man from the Garden of Eden to till the land from which he had been made. After driving the man out, at the entrance of the Garden of Eden he stationed angelic guards and a flaming, flashing sword to block the way to the tree of life.

A blocked path? No living here forever? The creator does a harsh thing. But it is also very good. What some may want will not be best for them. What others may want would not be right for them. Mercy and justice shake hands over a death pact, and angelic guards protect it.

We end with us. Here we are, as if in exile from paradise. We live, we love, and we labor. Later, we will leave. Other beings watch, and even intrude. Meanwhile, the serpent slithers about. Ever since the garden he has not stopped whispering, insinuating, and sometimes even shouting:

> *If God is God he is not good. And if God is good he is not God!*[28]

---

28 This is sometimes stated more prosaically as, "If God is all-powerful, he is not good. And if God is good, he is not all-powerful."

We are locked up in what appears to be exactly such a world. The jailer's words ring in our ears. But the saga tells us that, like the first couple, each of us must make up our mind about what the beast proclaims. There's no keeping him quiet, though we may try to avoid him with tricks of our own. We can plug our ears and busy ourselves to distraction. We can sing and dance and say "Look at what I can do!" Or we can lounge about, beer in hand, and belch, "Who cares?" But despite all our self-delusion, wherever we go it all smells like a dungeon.

If that's not a pleasant way to end this audacious little book, by all means please finish it yourself. In fact, that's precisely what the story is about, and exactly what the saga calls us to do. Hopefully, we'll heed its warnings and take heart from its encouragement. But even if you believe that all this spiritual stuff is a scam, you must still finish your own script. Write well, my fellow traveler!

Appendix

Bible Translations from Ancient Hebrew

To help us reflect upon the story of Adam and Eve, and our own lives with it, almost any existing English Bible will suffice. For those who know another language, a Bible in it will also do. Some, like the *King James Version*, are older and widely revered. Others use more modern terms and expressions. The approach to translation also varies. Some versions adhere more closely to Hebrew linguistic structures, others to natural English forms. Some serve religious communities, others are intended for a more secular audience. The issues are usually not a matter of right or wrong, but of purpose and audience.

Here are a couple of notes for the linguistically-minded, and also for those familiar with a particular English version.

Both vexing and beautiful is ancient Hebrew's lexicon, its stock of words. Like other so-called "Semitic" languages, Arabic being one, Hebrew words derive from a limited set of what are typically three-letter root forms. To them vowels and sometimes other consonants are added which branch out into a wide variety of spoken and written forms, the actual nouns, verbs, adjectives, participles, etc., of the language.

In addition, ancient Hebrew often used one word to mean many things. All languages do the same, but this is particularly true of ancient Hebrew, at least in the oldest form we have, the Hebrew Bible. On the one hand, it leaves us a comparatively limited number of words, and even fewer when considering their roots. But it also creates what might be called an especially "poetic" language, where an author can employ a single word or root to focus on a wide range of distinct yet similar meanings. Always swapping Hebrew words with a single English equivalent creates a seemingly simplistic, boring, and at times even confusing translation. But to not do so, at least in certain contexts, risks losing semantic strands created by repetition or paronomasia (puns) in the original author's tightly woven tapestry of meaning. Some of the key issues in Genesis 3 are discussed in the notes which accompany the translation presented here, and also in the chapters above.

A new translation of Genesis 3 was done specifically for this volume. Accuracy, clarity, and natural English were the goals, sometimes admittedly competing. The author worked directly from the best known and most widely used Hebrew source text, *Biblia Hebraica Stuttgartensia*, © 1967, 1977, 1983 Deutsche Bibelgesellschaft, Stuttgart. The translation is provided below in full, with notes explaining key issues. Chapter and verse numbers, not part of the original Hebrew text, are included.

A New Translation of Genesis Chapter 3

1 Of all the animals[a] the Eternal[b] God made, the serpent was the most cunning. And he asked the woman, "Can it be? Did God actually say, 'You two[c] must not eat from any of the garden trees'?"

> Note a, verse 1: The Hebrew reads *mkl xyt hsdh*, often translated something like "than all the beasts/animals of the field." But such a rendering could allow that some domestic animals (cf. verse 14 *hbhmh* often translated "cattle," "livestock," "domesticated animals") were more clever or cunning. The intent is that the serpent was supreme (with the possible understanding that wild animals are smarter than their domestic kin tamed and ruled by people). The translation "of all the animals" makes the meaning clear and unambiguous.

> Note b, verse 1: The Hebrew word here is the well-known *yhwh*, translated "LORD" in most English Bibles, even in the Jewish Publication Society's *The Tanakh* (whose title is an acronym for the *Torah* [the Pentateuch, or five books of Moses], *Nevi'im* [the Prophets], and *Kethuvim* [the Writings, such as the Psalms, Proverbs, Job, etc.], which together comprise what is commonly

known as the "Old Testament"). Though this is not the place to discuss the long history of the Hebrew word *yhwh* and its English translation, a couple of points should be noted. The Hebrew term is probably related to the verb for being or existence. Occurring first in Genesis 2:4, it is introduced as an addition to the term for deity, *'lhym*, used in Genesis 1 and usually translated "God." As such, *yhwh* points to God in relation to his creation. Unlike all others, he alone is the self-existent creator and covenant-keeping God of all people, and later of the Jews starting with Abraham (Exodus 3:13-15). English "LORD God" has some benefits, but it bows more to history than to the Hebrew text. This translation's use of "the Eternal God" attempts to more closely reflect the meaning of the original Hebrew.

Note c, verse 1: The Hebrew uses the second person plural form of the verb. English "you" is ambiguous, possibly meaning that only Eve could not eat the fruit. "You two" is more precise here, and so in verse 5. The original, divine form of this command is in Genesis 2:17, where "you" is singular and touching the fruit is not prohibited.

2 The woman responded, "We may eat fruit from the garden trees. 3 But God did say, 'You two must not eat fruit from the tree in the middle, or even touch it. If you do, you will die.'"

4 "You absolutely will not die!" the serpent replied. 5 "For God himself knows that the moment you two

eat from it your eyes will be opened. You will be like God,[d] enlightened[e] about good and bad, right and wrong!"[f]

> Note d, verse 5: The Hebrew word referring to the one true God is plural in form, and can also be used of lesser beings or false gods. As such, the text could be translated here "you will be like gods," an approach taken by a few English translations, if only in a footnote. Ultimately there would have been little difference in meaning to the first man and the woman (and thus for us). They had already been made in the image of God (Genesis 1:26-27). Becoming (more?) like God could mean to be like gods, and vice versa. For several reasons the term is translated here by the typical "God." First, there is thus far in the narrative no clear reference to other divine beings, at least none known to the man and the woman. Second, the term clearly means "God" from Genesis 1:1 to this point. Changing it to "gods," though theologically and linguistically possible, stretches the text beyond the setting of the garden story itself. Third, the serpent's temptation loses force by reference to lesser beings. Better instead to bait them with all he could, the very nature of God himself.

> Note e, verse 5: The Hebrew word here is *yd'y*, a very broad term referring to insight into, ability with, or intimate understanding of many things (e.g., see earlier in 3:5 "God ... knows," 3:7 "saw," 3:22 "experience," and 4:1, where Adam "knew"

Eve, meaning they had sexual relations). In English, "enlightened" correlates better both with the previous "eyes opened" and, in terms of usage, with the following "good and bad, right and wrong." When it came, at least, to eating fruit from the tree, the first man and woman knew the difference between right and wrong. The serpent was tempting them with something more than a limited, intellectual understanding.

Note f, verse 5: The Hebrew expression *twb wr'* is often translated "good and evil." While the Hebrew terms are both generic and used in a wide variety of expressions, the English terms are not. "Good" (especially as an adjective) can refer to excellence in morals, quality, ability, finances, health, weather, etc., whereas "evil" is almost exclusively restricted to the moral realm. The expanded translation here is intended to cover the wide range of both Hebrew terms.

6 Then the woman noticed that the tree's fruit was, in fact, good for food. It looked luscious and like a fount of wisdom. So she took some and ate it. And she handed some to her husband, who was with her, and he also ate it. 7 Then their eyes were opened. But what they saw[g] was their nakedness. So they sewed fig leaves together, making coverings for themselves.

Note g, verse 7: The word translated "saw" is from the same Hebrew root used in 3:5. See the related note there.

8 Later, during the cool time of day,[h] they heard the Eternal God in the garden. So there among its trees the man and his wife hid themselves from him. 9 But the Eternal God called out to the man, saying, "Where are you?"

> Note h, verse 8: Some have suggested the Hebrew *lrwx hywm* (wind or cool of the day) refers to God moving in a storm. But that understanding is unlikely. It was the man's sense of nakedness which caused him fear (verse 10), not any external commotion.

10 "I heard you in the garden," the man replied. "Because I was naked, I became afraid and hid myself."

11 The Eternal God then asked, "Who told you that you are naked? Have you eaten from the tree which I forbade?"

12 The man replied, "The woman you put here with me, she gave me fruit from the tree. So I ate it."

13 Then the Eternal God turned to the woman, "What's this you have done?"

She said, "The serpent deceived me, and I ate."

14 The Eternal God then addressed the serpent, "Because you did this, of all animals, domestic or wild, you are the most cursed. You will creep on your belly, licking dust every day of your life. 15 And I will make you and the woman enemies, likewise

your offspring and hers. Her offspring will strike your head, and you will strike her offspring's[i] heel."

> Note i, verse 15: The Hebrew nouns and their possessive suffixes zr'k and zr'h are most simply translated "your offspring/seed" and "her offspring/seed," singular in form but potentially plural in meaning. Also singular are the Hebrew pronouns in the second sentence, which might be more literally translated, "He will strike your head, and you will strike his heel." Translations done by Christians more often than not retain the grammatical singular form "he/his," whereas Jewish understanding tends toward the plural "they/their." The translation here has purposely slithered in between, using the somewhat tiresome repetition of "her offspring" in lieu of a singular or plural pronoun. Though the theological implications are potentially large either way, they are not dependent upon the grammatical number of the Hebrew or upon this verse alone. Furthermore, as is not uncommon in prophetic passages like this, the goal could be to encompass at least two different meanings to be fulfilled in distinct ways.

16 To the woman he said, "I will make childbearing very painful for you, and in pain you will give birth. You will want your husband, but he will rule over you."

17 And to Adam he said, "You did what your wife said—you ate from the tree which I forbade. Because

of you, the land[j] is now cursed. In pain you will survive on it all the days of your life. 18 It will give you thorns and thistles, and you'll eat what grows in its fields. 19 Your food will come by the sweat of your brow, until you return to the land from which you were made. For you are but dust, and to dust you will return."

> Note j, verse 17: The Hebrew term here and in verses 19 and 23, *h'dmh*, is closely related to the word for "man"/Adam. Often translated "the ground," it has sometimes been rendered "the land" or "the earth." Though distinct from *h'rc* (Genesis 1:1 and following), where "the earth" is opposed to "the heavens," in Jonah 4:2 it means "home" or "home country." The breadth of meaning inherent in English "land" (homeland, ground, real estate, natural resources, etc.) works well in this case.

20 Then the man named his wife Eve, for she would be the mother of all human life.

21 And the Eternal God made for Adam and his wife garments of skin and clothed them.

22 Then he said, "The man has now become like one of us, with experience[k] of right and wrong. He must not be allowed to also take and eat fruit from the tree of life, for then he would live forever!" 23 So the Eternal God banished the man from the Garden of Eden to till the land from which he had been made. 24 After driving the man out, at the entrance[l] of the Garden of Eden he stationed angelic guards and a

flaming, flashing sword to block the way to the tree of life.

> Note k, verse 22: The word "experience" is from the same Hebrew root used in 3:5. See the related note there.

> Note l, verse 24: Commonly translated "(at/to the) east," the Hebrew term *mqdm* is probably best understood here as "in front" or "at the entrance."

9 781945 413056